CRAFT Beer

by Douglas Yacka

MAD LIBS

An Imprint of Penguin Random House LLC, New York

Mad Libs format and text copyright © 2019 by Penguin Random House LLC. All rights reserved.

Concept created by Roger Price & Leonard Stern

Cover photograph: Rouzes/E+/Getty Images

Published by Mad Libs,
an imprint of Penguin Random House LLC, New York.
Printed in the USA.

Visit us online at www.penguinrandomhouse.com.

ISBN 9780593093597
13579108642

MAD LIBS® is a game for people who don't like games!
It can be played by one, two, three, four, or forty.

• RIDICULOUSLY SIMPLE DIRECTIONS

In this book, you'll find stories containing blank spaces where words are left out. One player, the READER, selects one of the stories. The READER shouldn't tell anyone what the story is about. Instead, the READER should ask the other players, the WRITERS, to give words to fill in the blank spaces in the story.

• TO PLAY

The READER asks each WRITER in turn to call out words—adjectives or nouns or whatever the spaces call for—and uses them to fill in the blank spaces in the story. The result is your very own MAD LIBS®! Then, when the READER reads the completed MAD LIBS® to the other players, they will discover they have written a story that is fantastic, screamingly funny, shocking, silly, crazy, or just plain dumb—depending on the words each WRITER called out.

• EXAMPLE (*Before* and *After*)

" _____ !" he said _____
       EXCLAMATION   ADVERB

as he jumped into his convertible _____ and
                            NOUN

drove off with his _____ wife.
              ADJECTIVE

" *Ouch* !" he said *happily*
       EXCLAMATION   ADVERB

as he jumped into his convertible *cat* and
                            NOUN

drove off with his *brave* wife.
              ADJECTIVE

In case you have forgotten what adjectives, adverbs, nouns, and verbs are, here is a quick review:

An **ADJECTIVE** describes something or somebody. _Lumpy, soft, ugly, messy,_ and _short_ are adjectives.

An **ADVERB** tells how something is done. It modifies a verb and usually ends in "ly." _Modestly, stupidly, greedily,_ and _carefully_ are adverbs.

A **NOUN** is the name of a person, place, or thing. _Sidewalk, umbrella, bridle, bathtub,_ and _nose_ are nouns.

A **VERB** is an action word. _Run, pitch, jump,_ and _swim_ are verbs. Put the verbs in past tense if the directions say **PAST TENSE**. _Ran, pitched, jumped,_ and _swam_ are verbs in the past tense.

When we ask for **A PLACE**, we mean any sort of place: a country or city (_Spain, Cleveland_) or a room (_bathroom, kitchen_).

An **EXCLAMATION** or **SILLY WORD** is any sort of funny sound, gasp, grunt, or outcry, like _Wow!, Ouch!, Whomp!, Ick!,_ and _Gadzooks!_

When we ask for specific words, like a **NUMBER**, a **COLOR**, an **ANIMAL**, or a **PART OF THE BODY**, we mean a word that is one of those things, like _seven, blue, horse,_ or _head._

When we ask for a **PLURAL**, it means more than one. For example, _cat_ pluralized is _cats._

MAD LIBS® is fun to play with friends, but you can also play it by yourself! To begin with, DO NOT look at the story on the page below. Fill in the blanks on this page with the words called for. Then, using the words you have selected, fill in the blank spaces in the story. Now you've created your own hilarious MAD LIBS® game!

VERB ENDING IN "ING" _____

VERB _____

NUMBER _____

ADJECTIVE _____

A PLACE _____

ADJECTIVE _____

VERB ENDING IN "ING" _____

NOUN _____

CELEBRITY _____

NOUN _____

ADJECTIVE _____

ADVERB _____

ADJECTIVE _____

ADJECTIVE _____

PLURAL NOUN _____

VERB _____

ADJECTIVE _____

TYPE OF EVENT _____

Calling all beer fans! This is the fight you've been _____ for.
VERB ENDING IN "ING"

This Sunday, Lager and Ale will _____ to the death in a battle
VERB

of foam and fervor! Weighing in at _____ pounds is Lager. Lean,
NUMBER

mean, and _____ , Lager fought its way up from the mean
ADJECTIVE

streets of (the) _____ to this very match today. After a long and
A PLACE

_____ fermentation, it began _____ into the crisp
ADJECTIVE   VERB ENDING IN "ING"

_____ we're ready to see fight! And let's not forget Lager's
NOUN

triumph last year when it pummeled _____ and took home the
CELEBRITY

_____ . On the other side of the ring is our _____
NOUN   ADJECTIVE

reigning champ, Ale! Fermented at the top, it _____ established
ADVERB

itself as a versatile fighter. From fruity to _____ to downright
ADJECTIVE

bitter, you never know what it will do next. Ask yourself, which version

of this _____ Ale will we see tonight? Who will be crowned
ADJECTIVE

the king of _____ ? Who will _____ in disgrace? Get
PLURAL NOUN   VERB

your _____ friends together, grab your openers, and let the
ADJECTIVE

_____ begin!
TYPE OF EVENT

MAD LIBS® is fun to play with friends, but you can also play it by yourself! To begin with, DO NOT look at the story on the page below. Fill in the blanks on this page with the words called for. Then, using the words you have selected, fill in the blank spaces in the story. Now you've created your own hilarious MAD LIBS® game!

PART OF THE BODY _____

PART OF THE BODY _____

PART OF THE BODY _____

ADJECTIVE _____

PLURAL NOUN _____

ADJECTIVE _____

ADVERB _____

ADJECTIVE _____

ADJECTIVE _____

ADJECTIVE _____

CELEBRITY _____

VERB ENDING IN "ING" _____

There's a lot more to beer than meets the _____. Let's
PART OF THE BODY

answer some FAQs:

Q: Should I leave the foam on top?

A: Yes! The foam (aka the _____) adds to the beer's texture
PART OF THE BODY

inside your _____. It can be fizzy, creamy, or even
PART OF THE BODY

_____ .
ADJECTIVE

Q: Should beer always be served cold?

A: It depends. Some _____ say that if it's too cold, you'll miss
PLURAL NOUN

the _____ flavors. As a tip, lagers are _____ served
ADJECTIVE   ADVERB

colder than ales. But by all means, dump that beer sitting out in the

_____ sun.
ADJECTIVE

Q: Is a beer hangover less _____ than a wine hangover?
ADJECTIVE

A: If you drink enough of either, you will be a/an _____ mess
ADJECTIVE

and stumble around like _____ before making a visit to the
CELEBRITY

toilet. Also, why are you _____ wine?
VERB ENDING IN "ING"

MAD LIBS® is fun to play with friends, but you can also play it by yourself! To begin with, DO NOT look at the story on the page below. Fill in the blanks on this page with the words called for. Then, using the words you have selected, fill in the blank spaces in the story. Now you've created your own hilarious MAD LIBS® game!

NOUN _____

PLURAL NOUN _____

SAME PLURAL NOUN _____

PLURAL NOUN _____

TYPE OF LIQUID _____

PART OF THE BODY _____

OCCUPATION (PLURAL) _____

PLURAL NOUN _____

ADJECTIVE _____

NOUN _____

VERB ENDING IN "ING" _____

PLURAL NOUN _____

ADJECTIVE _____

Students, let us begin. The birth of beer predates almost every historical

_____ you can think of. In fact, it is considered by many to be
NOUN

the first beverage made by _____ . When _____
PLURAL NOUN   SAME PLURAL NOUN

noticed the effect on grain when it came in contact with _____
PLURAL NOUN

in the air, they were mesmerized. They found that when they drank the

resulting _____ , it made their _____ feel good.
TYPE OF LIQUID   PART OF THE BODY

Evidence of beer making has been discovered in Mesopotamia by

_____ who found carvings of _____ in stone. Did
OCCUPATION (PLURAL)   PLURAL NOUN

you know it was the Egyptians who first recorded recipes on

_____ scrolls? Beer was used for religious ceremonies where
ADJECTIVE

the pharaoh would hold a/an _____ high in the air before
NOUN

_____ for all of his people to see. Some _____ even
VERB ENDING IN "ING"   PLURAL NOUN

believe it was buried in the pyramids with pharaohs after they died,

which must have made for some _____ mummies!
ADJECTIVE

The world's greatest _drinking_ game

MAD LIBS® is fun to play with friends, but you can also play it by yourself! To begin with, DO NOT look at the story on the page below. Fill in the blanks on this page with the words called for. Then, using the words you have selected, fill in the blank spaces in the story. Now you've created your own hilarious MAD LIBS® game!

PLURAL NOUN _____

ADJECTIVE _____

PERSON IN ROOM _____

ADJECTIVE _____

PERSON IN ROOM _____

NUMBER _____

NOUN _____

PLURAL NOUN _____

VERB ENDING IN "ING" _____

VERB _____

PLURAL NOUN _____

ADJECTIVE _____

ADJECTIVE _____

VERB _____

ADVERB _____

PART OF THE BODY _____

A PLACE _____

EXCLAMATION _____

Adult MAD LiBS®

RAISE YOUR GLASS (AND KEEP IT THERE)

The world's greatest *drinking* game

Ladies and _____ , may I have your attention, please!
PLURAL NOUN

As the best man, I will be toasting our _____ groom,
ADJECTIVE

_____ , and his _____ bride, _____ ,
PERSON IN ROOM ADJECTIVE PERSON IN ROOM

on their wedding day. In the _____ years I've known him, I never
NUMBER

thought he would actually find a/an _____ to accept him for
NOUN

his _____ . Growing up, I can't tell you how often he used
PLURAL NOUN

to spend all day _____ —it's still a shock to me someone
VERB ENDING IN "ING"

wanted to _____ him for life! He sure dated a lot of
VERB

_____ in the past, though. _____ ones,
PLURAL NOUN ADJECTIVE

_____ ones—he would pretty much _____ with
ADJECTIVE VERB

anyone. But then he _____ met the person who would capture
ADVERB

his _____ . I wish you both all the happiness in (the)
PART OF THE BODY

_____ . Let's all lift our glasses in the air and toast with a big
A PLACE

" _____ !"
EXCLAMATION

MAD LIBS® is fun to play with friends, but you can also play it by yourself! To begin with, DO NOT look at the story on the page below. Fill in the blanks on this page with the words called for. Then, using the words you have selected, fill in the blank spaces in the story. Now you've created your own hilarious MAD LIBS® game!

PART OF THE BODY _____

OCCUPATION _____

VERB ENDING IN "ING" _____

PLURAL NOUN _____

TYPE OF LIQUID _____

NOUN _____

NUMBER _____

ADJECTIVE _____

VERB ENDING IN "ING" _____

NOUN _____

TYPE OF CONTAINER _____

ADJECTIVE _____

NUMBER _____

VERB _____

ADJECTIVE _____

NUMBER _____

Adult MAD LiBS®

HOME-BREWING KIT INSTRUCTIONS

The world's greatest _drinking_ game

Are you ready to try your _____ at making your own
PART OF THE BODY

craft beer? You don't have to be a master _____ to do it
OCCUPATION

with this at-home kit!

- Start by _____ grains to release the natural
  VERB ENDING IN "ING"

  _____ inside.
  PLURAL NOUN

- Add hot _____ and heat until they become a/an
  TYPE OF LIQUID

  _____ -like mixture called "wort."
  NOUN

- Transfer the wort to a/an _____ -gallon kettle, and bring it
  NUMBER

  to a/an _____ boil, _____ your hops into
  ADJECTIVE   VERB ENDING IN "ING"

  the mix.

- Allow your _____ to cool off, add yeast, and pour into a
  NOUN

  sealed _____ . Put in a dark, _____ place.
  TYPE OF CONTAINER   ADJECTIVE

- After _____ weeks, it's time to filter your beer before you
  NUMBER

  _____ it into bottles.
  VERB

- Pop your home brews into the fridge, and get ready to taste your

  _____ work! Easy as one, two, _____ !
  ADJECTIVE   NUMBER

MAD LIBS® is fun to play with friends, but you can also play it by yourself! To begin with, DO NOT look at the story on the page below. Fill in the blanks on this page with the words called for. Then, using the words you have selected, fill in the blank spaces in the story. Now you've created your own hilarious MAD LIBS® game!

ADJECTIVE _____

ADJECTIVE _____

ADJECTIVE _____

PLURAL NOUN _____

ADVERB _____

PART OF THE BODY _____

PERSON IN ROOM _____

PLURAL NOUN _____

ANIMAL _____

CELEBRITY _____

COLOR _____

TYPE OF LIQUID _____

VERB ENDING IN "ING" _____

NOUN _____

ADJECTIVE _____

ADJECTIVE _____

Welcome to the Museum of Beer! I'll be guiding you through this

_____ exhibit of famous works inspired by the most
　　　ADJECTIVE

_____ of beverages. Our oldest painting is this _____
　　　ADJECTIVE　　　　　　　　　　　　　　　　　　　　　　　　　　ADJECTIVE

portrait of Zeus, the god of _____ . Look how _____
　　　　　　　　　　　　　　　PLURAL NOUN　　　　　　　　　　ADVERB

he holds the cup of beer high above his _____ . The
　　　　　　　　　　　　　　　　　　　　　　PART OF THE BODY

goddess _____ is seen to the right, carrying a basket of
　　　　　PERSON IN ROOM

_____ from the harvest for the next brew. The _____
　　PLURAL NOUN　　　　　　　　　　　　　　　　　　　　　　　　　ANIMAL

next to her represents beer's eternal goodness. Next is an Impressionist

piece by _____ . The artist captured beer's _____ color
　　　　　CELEBRITY　　　　　　　　　　　　　　　　　　　　COLOR

and foamy texture by mixing the paint with his own _____
　　　　　　　　　　　　　　　　　　　　　　　　　　　　TYPE OF LIQUID

and _____ his brush in a circular motion. Each piece of
　　　VERB ENDING IN "ING"

_____ in our collection is unique. Just look at this
　　　NOUN

_____ abstract work! Some call it _____ , but notice
　　ADJECTIVE　　　　　　　　　　　　　　　　　ADJECTIVE

how the completely blank canvas reminds you of beer? Now that's art.

Adult MAD LiBS

HIP HOPS

The world's greatest *drinking* game

MAD LIBS® is fun to play with friends, but you can also play it by yourself! To begin with, DO NOT look at the story on the page below. Fill in the blanks on this page with the words called for. Then, using the words you have selected, fill in the blank spaces in the story. Now you've created your own hilarious MAD LIBS® game!

NUMBER _____

ADJECTIVE _____

ADJECTIVE _____

PLURAL NOUN _____

ADJECTIVE _____

TYPE OF LIQUID _____

TYPE OF FOOD _____

VERB ENDING IN "ING" _____

ADJECTIVE _____

NOUN _____

NOUN _____

NUMBER _____

VERB _____

VERB _____

ADJECTIVE _____

ARTICLE OF CLOTHING (PLURAL) _____

OCCUPATION (PLURAL) _____

ANIMAL _____

Are you always on the hunt for a/an _____ percent beer with a/an
_____NUMBER_____

_____ flavor? If so, you are in _____ company. First,
ADJECTIVE   ADJECTIVE

a little history: Ancient _____ discovered that _____
                          PLURAL NOUN   ADJECTIVE

barley, yeast, and _____ made beer, but the result was often
                    TYPE OF LIQUID

sweeter than _____ . By _____ plants into the brew,
              TYPE OF FOOD   VERB ENDING IN "ING"

they were able to balance that sweetness . . . and eventually the IPA was

born. Thanks to the hop flower, we're able to enjoy this _____
                                                          ADJECTIVE

type of beer! Hops do more than add flavor to the _____ ; they
                                                    NOUN

also give off different aromas at the end of the brewing process.

Common smells include citrus, _____ , and grass. With at
                               NOUN

least _____ types of hops, there are so many possibilities to
       NUMBER

_____ . American craft brewers like to _____ with lots
VERB   VERB

of hops, resulting in _____ beers that can knock your
                       ADJECTIVE

_____ off! And let's not forget, _____ recently
ARTICLE OF CLOTHING (PLURAL)   OCCUPATION (PLURAL)

confirmed that hops are related to the cannabis plant. Maybe Snoop

_____ would dig drinking an IPA with you.
ANIMAL

MAD LIBS® is fun to play with friends, but you can also play it by yourself! To begin with, DO NOT look at the story on the page below. Fill in the blanks on this page with the words called for. Then, using the words you have selected, fill in the blank spaces in the story. Now you've created your own hilarious MAD LIBS® game!

ADJECTIVE _____

PLURAL NOUN _____

ADJECTIVE _____

COLOR _____

TYPE OF LIQUID _____

PLURAL NOUN _____

ADJECTIVE _____

ADJECTIVE _____

ANIMAL (PLURAL) _____

ADJECTIVE _____

ANIMAL _____

ADJECTIVE _____

VERB ENDING IN "ING" _____

TYPE OF BUILDING (PLURAL) _____

PLURAL NOUN _____

ADJECTIVE _____

PART OF THE BODY (PLURAL) _____

Welcome back, beer nerds! By the Middle Ages, ale was a/an

_____ part of the daily diet. It was actually the main way
ADJECTIVE

_____ stayed hydrated, thanks to _____
PLURAL NOUN   ADJECTIVE

_____ water that tasted like _____. While kings and
COLOR   TYPE OF LIQUID

noble _____ indulged in fine wine, beer was definitely a part
PLURAL NOUN

of their _____ feasts as well. The knights of the _____
ADJECTIVE   ADJECTIVE

Table would drink after jousting on their trusty _____. For
ANIMAL (PLURAL)

the common folk, beer was a/an _____ source of nutrition,
ADJECTIVE

especially if they couldn't afford a/an _____ to roast. It also
ANIMAL

helped them forget how _____ and depressing their lives
ADJECTIVE

were. Monks began _____ special beers in their
VERB ENDING IN "ING"

_____. Some of these ales were flavored with spices and
TYPE OF BUILDING (PLURAL)

_____. These _____ ales were so high in alcohol, the
PLURAL NOUN   ADJECTIVE

monks put their sandals on the wrong _____!
PART OF THE BODY (PLURAL)

MAD LIBS® is fun to play with friends, but you can also play it by yourself! To begin with, DO NOT look at the story on the page below. Fill in the blanks on this page with the words called for. Then, using the words you have selected, fill in the blank spaces in the story. Now you've created your own hilarious MAD LIBS® game!

ADJECTIVE _____

ADJECTIVE _____

ADJECTIVE _____

PLURAL NOUN _____

ADJECTIVE _____

VERB _____

PLURAL NOUN _____

TYPE OF LIQUID _____

VERB ENDING IN "ING" _____

ADJECTIVE _____

VERB ENDING IN "ING" _____

COUNTRY _____

ADJECTIVE _____

PART OF THE BODY _____

TYPE OF FOOD _____

EXCLAMATION _____

LETTER OF THE ALPHABET _____

Welcome to my site, fellow snobs! If you came searching for reviews of

the world's most _____ beverage, look no further. Check out
                  ADJECTIVE

my _____ reviews below.
   ADJECTIVE

• Hoppy Birthday IPA: Smelled like a/an _____ bouquet of
                                         ADJECTIVE

_____ . It was so _____ on the palate, I could
PLURAL NOUN   ADJECTIVE

_____ . Rating: C
VERB

• 3 _____ Brewery Belgian-Style: If you crossed a Belgian
     PLURAL NOUN

tripel with _____ , this is what you'd get. A bit iffy at first,
             TYPE OF LIQUID

but then it began _____ on my tongue. What a/an
                   VERB ENDING IN "ING"

_____ surprise! Rating: B+
ADJECTIVE

• Sandy's Summer Sipper: This was so citrusy, I might as well have

been _____ a lemon. Rating: D
     VERB ENDING IN "ING"

• Bock to the Future: Instantly transported me to _____
                                                   COUNTRY

with its assertive _____ aromas. This one totally blew my
                    ADJECTIVE

_____ ! Rating: A+
PART OF THE BODY

• Old-School _____ Stout: _____ ! 'Nuff said.
              TYPE OF FOOD   EXCLAMATION

Rating: _____
        LETTER OF THE ALPHABET

MAD LIBS® is fun to play with friends, but you can also play it by yourself! To begin with, DO NOT look at the story on the page below. Fill in the blanks on this page with the words called for. Then, using the words you have selected, fill in the blank spaces in the story. Now you've created your own hilarious MAD LIBS® game!

ADJECTIVE _____

VERB ENDING IN "ING" _____

ADJECTIVE _____

NOUN _____

COLOR _____

ADJECTIVE _____

ANIMAL _____

NUMBER _____

PART OF THE BODY _____

OCCUPATION (PLURAL) _____

VERB _____

CELEBRITY _____

PART OF THE BODY _____

TYPE OF FOOD _____

TYPE OF LIQUID _____

ADVERB _____

To my _____ fans,
_{ADJECTIVE}

It's your old pal Beer here. It has come to my attention that many of

you have been _____ with other beverages lately. I can't tell
_{VERB ENDING IN "ING"}

you how _____ this makes me feel. It seems that wine is the
_{ADJECTIVE}

_____ of choice for some. White, red, or _____ , it's all
_{NOUN} _{COLOR}

_____ if you ask me! Could you imagine pairing wine with a
_{ADJECTIVE}

hot _____ ? Gross! Fancy cocktails with _____ ingredients
_{ANIMAL} _{NUMBER}

are in style, too. Bartenders who wear garters on their _____
_{PART OF THE BODY}

and call themselves _____ make me want to _____ .
_{OCCUPATION (PLURAL)} _{VERB}

And even though _____ endorses a certain tequila, it's still not
_{CELEBRITY}

cool to lick salt off your _____ , do a shot, and then suck
_{PART OF THE BODY}

on a/an _____ . You know what doesn't need a chaser? Beer,
_{TYPE OF FOOD}

that's what! This really has to stop, people. What's next, _____ ?!
_{TYPE OF LIQUID}

Yours _____ ,
_{ADVERB}

Beer

MAD LIBS® is fun to play with friends, but you can also play it by yourself! To begin with, DO NOT look at the story on the page below. Fill in the blanks on this page with the words called for. Then, using the words you have selected, fill in the blank spaces in the story. Now you've created your own hilarious MAD LIBS® game!

ADJECTIVE _____

ADVERB _____

VERB ENDING IN "ING" _____

TYPE OF LIQUID _____

ADJECTIVE _____

TYPE OF FOOD (PLURAL) _____

ANIMAL _____

ADJECTIVE _____

COLOR _____

COUNTRY _____

PART OF THE BODY _____

NUMBER _____

VERB _____

ANIMAL _____

TYPE OF FOOD _____

VERB _____

TYPE OF FOOD _____

EXCLAMATION _____

Some folks chug their beer with _____ bar snacks, but beer

ADJECTIVE

pairs _____ with fine cuisine, too. Try _____ a crisp

ADVERB

VERB ENDING IN "ING"

pale ale instead of _____ during cocktail hour. Oysters on

TYPE OF LIQUID

the _____ shell, _____ wrapped in bacon, and

ADJECTIVE

TYPE OF FOOD (PLURAL)

even _____ liver pâté pair well with this type of brew.

ANIMAL

A/An _____ hefeweizen is perfectly matched with a fresh

ADJECTIVE

_____ salad. And if you serve onion soup from _____,

COLOR

COUNTRY

a brown ale will put a smile on your _____. For the main

PART OF THE BODY

course, there are no less than _____ choices of beer pairings. A

NUMBER

savory saison will _____ your chicken à la king. _____

VERB

ANIMAL

confit calls for a rich Belgian tripel. In the chilly months, a hearty

_____ stew and a porter are the perfect pair. And don't forget

TYPE OF FOOD

dessert! Chocolate soufflé and a double ale _____ together

VERB

delightfully. But a fruity lambic with your _____ tart is sure to

TYPE OF FOOD

leave your guests cheering "_____!"

EXCLAMATION

MAD LIBS® is fun to play with friends, but you can also play it by yourself! To begin with, DO NOT look at the story on the page below. Fill in the blanks on this page with the words called for. Then, using the words you have selected, fill in the blank spaces in the story. Now you've created your own hilarious MAD LIBS® game!

ADJECTIVE _____

COUNTRY _____

NOUN _____

TYPE OF FOOD _____

PLURAL NOUN _____

TYPE OF LIQUID _____

PLURAL NOUN _____

ADJECTIVE _____

PLURAL NOUN _____

VERB _____

ADJECTIVE _____

NUMBER _____

TYPE OF FOOD (PLURAL) _____

VERB _____

ADJECTIVE _____

VERB ENDING IN "ING" _____

ADJECTIVE _____

It's our final lesson of the day, _____ students! Beer

ADJECTIVE

drinking, as we know it today, can be traced back to the pubs of Olde

_____ . _____ sellers in the city, _____

COUNTRY   NOUN   TYPE OF FOOD

farmers in the countryside, and everyone in between would meet at

local pubs with their _____ after work for a pint of

PLURAL NOUN

_____ . Over mugs of beer, folks would laugh about their

TYPE OF LIQUID

_____ , cry about their _____ jobs, and share their

PLURAL NOUN   ADJECTIVE

hopes and _____ . Bar owners soon realized that people were

PLURAL NOUN

more likely to _____ at their establishments if they offered

VERB

_____ specials in the early evening, like _____-for-one

ADJECTIVE   NUMBER

drinks. Often, snacks like pretzels and _____ were placed on

TYPE OF FOOD (PLURAL)

the bar so patrons could _____ while they drank. This convivial

VERB

time soon became known as "_____ hour." The next time

ADJECTIVE

you're out _____ with your friends, remember that you are

VERB ENDING IN "ING"

carrying on a/an _____ tradition. Cheers!

ADJECTIVE

MAD LIBS® is fun to play with friends, but you can also play it by yourself! To begin with, DO NOT look at the story on the page below. Fill in the blanks on this page with the words called for. Then, using the words you have selected, fill in the blank spaces in the story. Now you've created your own hilarious MAD LIBS® game!

ADJECTIVE _____

PERSON IN ROOM _____

VERB ENDING IN "ING" _____

A PLACE _____

ANIMAL (PLURAL) _____

PART OF THE BODY (PLURAL) _____

ADJECTIVE _____

NUMBER _____

NOUN _____

PART OF THE BODY (PLURAL) _____

PLURAL NOUN _____

ADVERB _____

TYPE OF BUILDING _____

ADJECTIVE _____

VERB _____

SILLY WORD _____

ADJECTIVE _____

VERB ENDING IN "ING" _____

Adult MAD LiBS® WE TOTALLY MADE BEER

The world's greatest _drinking_ game

Welcome to the _____ opening of our brewery, dudes and
               ADJECTIVE

dudettes! My best buddy, _____, and I have been
                           PERSON IN ROOM

_____ about this since we met at the University of
VERB ENDING IN "ING"

_____. That's right—home of the Fighting _____!
  A PLACE   ANIMAL (PLURAL)

After graduation, we decided to put our _____ together
                                       PART OF THE BODY (PLURAL)

and make our _____ dream come true. Plus, my dad gave us
                ADJECTIVE

_____ dollars in seed money. We read every _____ about
 NUMBER   NOUN

beer we could get our _____ on, and ordered all of the
                   PART OF THE BODY (PLURAL)

_____ we needed to start brewing. _____, we
  PLURAL NOUN   ADVERB

rented this righteous _____ for our brewery headquarters.
                     TYPE OF BUILDING

Please try some _____ samples of our beer. I hope you
                 ADJECTIVE

_____ it as much as we do. Oh, _____! We totally
 VERB   SILLY WORD

forgot to think of a/an _____ name for our new brewery!
                     ADJECTIVE

How about Two Friends _____ Company?
                 VERB ENDING IN "ING"

MAD LIBS® is fun to play with friends, but you can also play it by yourself! To begin with, DO NOT look at the story on the page below. Fill in the blanks on this page with the words called for. Then, using the words you have selected, fill in the blank spaces in the story. Now you've created your own hilarious MAD LIBS® game!

NOUN _____

ADJECTIVE _____

ADJECTIVE _____

COLOR _____

ADJECTIVE _____

PART OF THE BODY _____

PLURAL NOUN _____

TYPE OF FOOD _____

ADJECTIVE _____

PLURAL NOUN _____

NOUN _____

ADVERB _____

VERB _____

VERB _____

TYPE OF FOOD _____

ADJECTIVE _____

PERSON IN ROOM _____

PLURAL NOUN _____

If you pop open a beer and start drinking right away, you're missing

half the _____. Evaluating beer is just as _____
          NOUN   ADJECTIVE

as tasting a fine wine. Begin by examining the color. Is it a/an

_____ shade of gold or a dark _____? Does it have a
   ADJECTIVE   COLOR

large or _____ amount of foam? Next, put your
              ADJECTIVE

_____ into the glass. What sort of _____ do you
PART OF THE BODY   PLURAL NOUN

smell? Freshly baked _____, perhaps? _____ spices?
                     TYPE OF FOOD   ADJECTIVE

A bouquet of _____? You might even detect notes of
             PLURAL NOUN

_____. Now _____ take a sip and _____ it
   NOUN   ADVERB   VERB

around in your mouth. You should feel it _____ on each area
                                          VERB

of your tongue. Is it sour like a/an _____? _____ like
                                     TYPE OF FOOD   ADJECTIVE

dessert? Does the bitterness remind you of _____? Now
                                           PERSON IN ROOM

you're a tasting pro who can impress all of the _____ at the
                                                PLURAL NOUN

alehouse.

Adult MAD LiBS®

YOU KNOW YOU'VE HAD TOO MUCH BEER WHEN . . .

The world's greatest _drinking_ game

MAD LIBS® is fun to play with friends, but you can also play it by yourself! To begin with, DO NOT look at the story on the page below. Fill in the blanks on this page with the words called for. Then, using the words you have selected, fill in the blank spaces in the story. Now you've created your own hilarious MAD LIBS® game!

NOUN _____

NUMBER _____

PART OF THE BODY _____

VERB ENDING IN "ING" _____

NUMBER _____

TYPE OF FOOD _____

PLURAL NOUN _____

OCCUPATION _____

PART OF THE BODY _____

ADJECTIVE _____

VERB _____

CELEBRITY _____

A PLACE _____

TYPE OF BUILDING _____

COUNTRY _____

Beer is a whole lot of _____ when consumed in moderation.

NOUN

But you know you've had one or _____ too many when:

NUMBER

- You text your ex that you miss their beautiful _____ .

PART OF THE BODY

- Your _____ makes the neighbors complain.

VERB ENDING IN "ING"

- You leave a/an _____ -dollar tip for the bartender.

NUMBER

- You binge eat every _____ in your kitchen.

TYPE OF FOOD

- You have trouble finding the _____ to open your front door.

PLURAL NOUN

- You enroll in an online course to become a/an _____ .

OCCUPATION

- You wake up the next morning with your _____ throbbing.

PART OF THE BODY

- You start telling the long, _____ story of how you learned to _____ .

ADJECTIVE / VERB

- You start doing the _____ impression that your friends all hate.

CELEBRITY

- You are no longer welcome back in (the) _____ . Or the _____ . Or _____ .

A PLACE / TYPE OF BUILDING / COUNTRY

MAD LIBS® is fun to play with friends, but you can also play it by yourself! To begin with, DO NOT look at the story on the page below. Fill in the blanks on this page with the words called for. Then, using the words you have selected, fill in the blank spaces in the story. Now you've created your own hilarious MAD LIBS® game!

PLURAL NOUN _____

NOUN _____

NOUN _____

PLURAL NOUN _____

FIRST NAME _____

NOUN _____

CITY _____

SILLY WORD _____

PLURAL NOUN _____

PLURAL NOUN _____

COLOR _____

NOUN _____

ADVERB _____

ADJECTIVE _____

PLURAL NOUN _____

NUMBER _____

LEADER OF THE (SIX) PACK

The world's greatest _drinking_ game

What is the most popular beer in the United _____ of America?

PLURAL NOUN

Many would name a big brand like _____-weiser, known as

NOUN

the "_____ of Beers." It is, after all, consumed by millions of

NOUN

_____ all across the country. However, New Englanders might

PLURAL NOUN

argue that _____ Adams is America's beer, since it's named

FIRST NAME

for a patriot who signed the _____ of Independence. Westerners

NOUN

from _____ might suggest _____ Light, with the

CITY   SILLY WORD

classic ad campaign "Cold as the _____." The most famous

PLURAL NOUN

Irish stout has many devoted American _____ as well. With its

PLURAL NOUN

dark _____ shade and creamy _____ on top, it's

COLOR   NOUN

easy to spot. These days, there are _____ hundreds of

ADVERB

_____ craft brews, so the fight for most popular will be debated

ADJECTIVE

by _____ for years to come. One thing we can all agree on:

PLURAL NOUN

Let's open _____ more beers!

NUMBER

MAD LIBS® is fun to play with friends, but you can also play it by yourself! To begin with, DO NOT look at the story on the page below. Fill in the blanks on this page with the words called for. Then, using the words you have selected, fill in the blank spaces in the story. Now you've created your own hilarious MAD LIBS® game!

ADJECTIVE _____

VERB _____

ADJECTIVE _____

PLURAL NOUN _____

NOUN _____

ADJECTIVE _____

NUMBER _____

ANIMAL _____

VEHICLE _____

TYPE OF BUILDING _____

ARTICLE OF CLOTHING _____

ADJECTIVE _____

PLURAL NOUN _____

VERB _____

CELEBRITY _____

PART OF THE BODY (PLURAL) _____

Adult MAD LiBS®   THE BEER ZODIAC

The world's greatest _drinking_ game

Beer isn't just a drink—it has many mystical and _____
                                                    ADJECTIVE

properties. What does your favorite type of beer _____ about
                                                      VERB

you?

- As the _____ saying goes, blondes have more fun. That is
         ADJECTIVE

  certainly true for _____ who adore blonde ales.
                      PLURAL NOUN

- Amber aficionado, you prefer a quiet night at home, curled up on

  the _____ with a/an _____ book. You're probably
         NOUN   ADJECTIVE

  asleep by _____ o'clock.
             NUMBER

- IPA fan, you are one cool _____. You probably drive a
                              ANIMAL

  fancy _____ , live in a deluxe _____ , and wear the
          VEHICLE   TYPE OF BUILDING

  most fashionable _____ .
                    ARTICLE OF CLOTHING

- Stout folks are the _____ , silent type. The _____
                        ADJECTIVE   PLURAL NOUN

  in your life can always count on you to _____ for them
                                               VERB

  when it matters.

- And of course, pilsners make the best lovers. You have as much

  swagger as _____ and break _____ wherever
              CELEBRITY   PART OF THE BODY (PLURAL)

  you go.

MAD LIBS® is fun to play with friends, but you can also play it by yourself! To begin with, DO NOT look at the story on the page below. Fill in the blanks on this page with the words called for. Then, using the words you have selected, fill in the blank spaces in the story. Now you've created your own hilarious MAD LIBS® game!

ADJECTIVE _____

NUMBER _____

VERB _____

VERB ENDING IN "ING" _____

NOUN _____

PLURAL NOUN _____

NOUN _____

CELEBRITY _____

ADVERB _____

ANIMAL _____

TYPE OF FOOD (PLURAL) _____

ADJECTIVE _____

It's a close call, but beer is definitely better and more _____
ADJECTIVE

than sex. Here's why:

1. You can drink beer for _____ hours without getting worn-out.
   NUMBER

2. There's no need to _____ yourself in the shower before beer.
   VERB

3. You can enjoy _____ with all your friends.
   VERB ENDING IN "ING"

4. Beer doesn't care that you look like a/an _____ when you
   NOUN

   wake up.

5. _____ don't mind beer in public places.
   PLURAL NOUN

6. You can talk about beers you've had in the past with your

   _____-in-law.
   NOUN

7. _____ wouldn't appear in an ad for sex.
   CELEBRITY

8. Whether you drink quickly or _____, no one is
   ADVERB

   disappointed.

9. Beer is great with a/an _____ burger and _____ .
   ANIMAL   TYPE OF FOOD (PLURAL)

   Sex, not so much.

10. You aren't expected to send a/an _____ text the day after
    ADJECTIVE

    beer.

MAD LIBS® is fun to play with friends, but you can also play it by yourself! To begin with, DO NOT look at the story on the page below. Fill in the blanks on this page with the words called for. Then, using the words you have selected, fill in the blank spaces in the story. Now you've created your own hilarious MAD LIBS® game!

ADJECTIVE _____

VERB ENDING IN "S" _____

ADJECTIVE _____

ANIMAL (PLURAL) _____

COLOR _____

ADVERB _____

ANIMAL _____

CELEBRITY _____

VERB ENDING IN "ING" _____

ADJECTIVE _____

PLURAL NOUN _____

ARTICLE OF CLOTHING _____

CELEBRITY _____

PART OF THE BODY _____

VERB _____

NOUN _____

VERB ENDING IN "ING" _____

NOUN _____

Lights up on a wide shot of the _____ prairie. Wind
_____(ADJECTIVE)_____ through fields with _____ mountains in the
___(VERB ENDING IN "S")___   (ADJECTIVE)
background. A flock of _____ soar through the bright
                        (ANIMAL (PLURAL))
_____ sky. A cowboy, _____ riding his
(COLOR)   (ADVERB)
_____, comes into view. Close-up of cowboy. He has that
(ANIMAL)
rugged look, like _____. The prairie sun is _____
                   (CELEBRITY)   (VERB ENDING IN "ING")
down on him, and he is hot. Cut to a/an _____ saloon. The
                                         (ADJECTIVE)
cowboy walks through the swinging _____, takes off his
                                    (PLURAL NOUN)
_____, and finds a seat at the bar. The bartender, ideally
(ARTICLE OF CLOTHING)
played by _____, asks him what he'd like to drink. Close-up of
          (CELEBRITY)
the cowboy's _____ as he says, "I only _____ one
             (PART OF THE BODY)   (VERB)
kind of beer. All-American." He takes a big _____ from the
                                             (NOUN)
bottle and smiles. Cut to cowboy _____ into the distance.
                                  (VERB ENDING IN "ING")
Close-up shot of a beer bottle with the logo of a/an _____
                                                      (NOUN)
holding a flag.

MAD LIBS® is fun to play with friends, but you can also play it by yourself! To begin with, DO NOT look at the story on the page below. Fill in the blanks on this page with the words called for. Then, using the words you have selected, fill in the blank spaces in the story. Now you've created your own hilarious MAD LIBS® game!

PLURAL NOUN _____

TYPE OF FOOD _____

VERB ENDING IN "ING" _____

ADJECTIVE _____

ADVERB _____

NOUN _____

PART OF THE BODY _____

TYPE OF CONTAINER _____

ADJECTIVE _____

VERB ENDING IN "ING" _____

VERB _____

ADJECTIVE _____

NOUN _____

PART OF THE BODY _____

ADJECTIVE _____

EXCLAMATION _____

NUMBER _____

There is more to the tale of "Goldilocks and the Three Bears" than

most _____ know. Many years after eating the bears'
     PLURAL NOUN

_____ and _____ in their beds, Goldilocks, now a
TYPE OF FOOD   VERB ENDING IN "ING"

grown-up, found herself lost in the same _____ forest. She
                                          ADJECTIVE

came upon the same cottage and _____ sneaked inside. Feeling
                                ADVERB

thirsty, Goldilocks opened the refrigerator _____ . Inside was
                                             NOUN

every type of beer her _____ could desire. She opened the
                       PART OF THE BODY

first _____ and took a sip. "This beer is too _____!"
      TYPE OF CONTAINER   ADJECTIVE

she declared before _____ it into the sink. She grabbed the
                    VERB ENDING IN "ING"

next bottle and began to _____ . "This beer is too
                         VERB

_____!" she whined, and dumped it on the _____ .
ADJECTIVE   NOUN

She opened one more beer. A smile crossed her _____ .
                                              PART OF THE BODY

"This beer is simply _____!" Just then, the three bears arrived
                     ADJECTIVE

home. "_____!" yelled Mama Bear. "Is that Goldilocks
       EXCLAMATION

again?" But rather than eat her, the bears had Goldilocks arrested. She

is currently serving five to _____ years in prison.
                             NUMBER

MAD LIBS® is fun to play with friends, but you can also play it by yourself! To begin with, DO NOT look at the story on the page below. Fill in the blanks on this page with the words called for. Then, using the words you have selected, fill in the blank spaces in the story. Now you've created your own hilarious MAD LIBS® game!

ADVERB _____

ADJECTIVE _____

TYPE OF FOOD _____

PART OF THE BODY _____

PLURAL NOUN _____

OCCUPATION (PLURAL) _____

VERB ENDING IN "ING" _____

COLOR _____

PLURAL NOUN _____

ADJECTIVE _____

SILLY WORD _____

CELEBRITY _____

VERB ENDING IN "ING" _____

PLURAL NOUN _____

NUMBER _____

TO YOUR HEALTH!

The world's greatest _drinking_ game

As your doctor, I _____ recommend making some

ADVERB

_____ changes to your diet. A/An _____ a day may

ADJECTIVE   TYPE OF FOOD

keep me away, but if you really want to stay healthy, drink beer. Recent

studies show that a pint a day reduces the risk of _____

PART OF THE BODY

disease by keeping your _____ in check. _____ have

PLURAL NOUN   OCCUPATION (PLURAL)

also found that it keeps your bones from _____, which is

VERB ENDING IN "ING"

important as you grow old and _____. Antioxidants in beer

COLOR

help eliminate _____ from your body, so you can wake up

PLURAL NOUN

feeling _____. Beer is full of nutrients as well, like potassium,

ADJECTIVE

magnesium, and _____. Ever wonder why _____

SILLY WORD   CELEBRITY

looks so young? You guessed it! And of course, after a long day of

_____, beer can help your body relax by releasing the

VERB ENDING IN "ING"

_____ in your brain that make you feel good.

PLURAL NOUN

My prescription: Drink _____ and call me in the morning.

NUMBER

Download Mad Libs today!

Join the millions of Mad Libs fans creating wacky and wonderful stories on our apps!